CLASSIC WIS

TODAY'S QUESTIONS. TIMELESS ANSWERS.

Looking for time-tested guidance for the dilemmas of the spiritual life? Find it in the company of the wise spiritual masters of our Catholic tradition.

Comfort in Hardship: Wisdom from Thérèse of Lisieux

Inner Peace: Wisdom from Jean-Pierre de Caussade

Life's Purpose: Wisdom from John Henry Newman

Path of Holiness: Wisdom from Catherine of Siena

Peace in Prayer: Wisdom from Teresa of Avila

Secrets of the Spirit: Wisdom from Luis Martinez

A Simple Life: Wisdom from Jane Frances de Chantal

Solace in Suffering: Wisdom from Thomas à Kempis

Strength in Darkness: Wisdom from John of the Cross

Forthcoming volumes will include wisdom from:
Francis de Sales

Secrets of the Spirit

CLASSIC WISDOM COLLECTION

Secrets of the Spirit

Wisdom from Luis Martinez

Edited and with a Foreword by Germana Santos, FSP

BOOKS & MEDIA
Boston

Library of Congress Cataloging-in-Publication Data

Martínez, Luis M. (Luis Maria), 1881-1956.
  [Selections. English]
  Secrets of the Spirit : wisdom from Luis Martinez / edited and with a
foreword by Germana Santos.
      p. cm. -- (Classic wisdom collection)
  Includes bibliographical references.
  ISBN 0-8198-7150-8 (pbk.)
  1. Spiritual life--Catholic Church. I. Santos, Germana. II. Title.
  BX2350.3.M274213 2011
  248.4'82--dc22

                        2010049475

Cover design by Rosana Usselmann

Cover photo by Mary Emmanuel Alves, FSP

Published by Pauline Books & Media, 50 Saint Pauls Avenue, Boston, MA 02130-3491

Printed in the U.S.A.

www.pauline.org

Pauline Books & Media is the publishing house of the Daughters of St. Paul, an international congregation of women religious serving the Church with the communications media.

1 2 3 4 5 6 7 8 9   15 14 13 12 11

In gratitude to my religious community,
the Daughters of Saint Paul,
and to my family and friends,
who prayerfully and lovingly walked with me
during my recent "cancer journey"
and to the medical staff
of Saint Elizabeth's Medical Center of Boston
who, through their wonderful care and positive attitude,
made my journey more bearable

Contents

Notes

Sources

Foreword

Archbishop Luis Maria Martinez (1881–1956) was a popular spiritual writer in his day, and even today his writings continue to inspire us. He lived in Mexico during very turbulent years, when the Church was persecuted by a militant anti-Catholic government. Despite all this, Martinez carried out a successful ministry and he spent the last nineteen years of his life wisely guiding his people as primate archbishop of Mexico City.

When I saw his picture I liked his joyful smile and the cheerful glint in his eyes. Martinez was known for having a good sense of humor, and some of his contemporaries even thought of him as too lighthearted. But beneath the good humor, he was a man of deep spirituality and mysticism, and a dedicated spiritual guide to his people, endowed with wise social and political abilities. His rich and holy life is now under review during the process of canonization.

When I read *The Sanctifier*, Martinez's classic book on the Holy Spirit, I was moved by his poetic language and consoling message of God's care and goodness. At that time I needed this encouraging message more than ever. My mother had recently died after living with Alzheimer's disease for several years. I had cared for her during the last few years of her life. Although I believe that her death was a gentle deliverance from her suffering as she entrusted her soul to God, it left a void in my life and the lives of my family members.

One month later I was diagnosed with cancer, which derailed my own life's plans. I initially responded with shock and disbelief, followed by denial of the seriousness of the cancer. I expected to sail through surgery and recuperate quickly, in order to start an exciting new assignment overseas. But my denial was shot through with the news that I would need six months of chemotherapy, two months of radiation, and later six more months of a clinical trial medication.

The year-long journey of treatment and recovery taught me many lessons. As a woman religious I had been praying several hours daily for many years, but I was confronted with a challenging season in my prayer and interior life. I had thought that when I was sick and needed God's help and protection the most, I would be able to pray more. Instead, the discomforting effects of chemotherapy and radiation affected me physically, emotionally, and spiritually, so that prayer was often more of a burden than a consolation.

At those times when my physical strength lagged and my spirit felt like a small boat adrift without a compass on the wide sea, I was given the gift of being supported and uplifted by the sisters of my community as they gathered daily in chapel to raise their voices in prayer. Sometimes silently or in a weak whisper, I united myself to this chorus of praise and felt strengthened by this communion.

On many days, my time of adoration before the Blessed Sacrament consisted in simply "showing up," in being present without too many words or lofty thoughts, trusting that Jesus Master accepted my desire to pray. He, himself, is always offering us his own unfailing, silent, comforting presence in the Eucharist. The Rosary, with its gentle rhythm of Hail Marys, became a reassuring prayer as I reflected on Jesus's life and Mary's response of faith. I found great benefit in reading Scripture and a few spiritual books. In this regard, whenever I opened *The Sanctifier*, I was never disappointed. Martinez's profound message, vested in rich, lyrical writing, provided the words that I needed for prayer, and the courage to face my ordeal.

Although prayer and the interior life demanded more effort during my illness, I didn't think of giving them up. At that most vulnerable time, when my usually healthy body struggled with a silent, destructive enemy, I pondered life's deep questions. Death had always been an elusive thought in the midst of my very active life. But faced with the concrete awareness that death is inescapable, the core of my being focused on essentials. In those times, the idea of my detailed *curriculum vitae* describing works, travels, diplomas, roles, and activities faded into insignificance compared to a simple life spent in union with Jesus Christ, seeking holiness through selfless ministry to others.

During that period of introspection resulting from my illness and the awareness of life's precariousness, I appreciated having the writings of Archbishop Martinez as consoling and secure guidance.

Luis Maria Martinez was born on January 9, 1881, in Michoacan, Mexico. The joy of his birth was clouded eleven days later by the death of his father, Rosendo Martinez. Suddenly widowed, Ramona Rodriguez cared lovingly for her son, and relied on her brothers to be a paternal influence for the young boy. His two uncles, one of them a priest, passed on to young Luis a love of nature and the disciplined and manly traits that characterized his entire life.

At an especially young age, Luis Maria entered the seminary on January 2, 1891. He was ordained a priest on November 20, 1904. He was soon named professor of the seminary in Morelia, in the state of Michoacan, then vice rector, and eventually rector of the same seminary.

It became obvious to those who knew him that this young priest possessed the gifts of intelligence, leadership, and rich spiritual acuity and devotion. In quick succession he attained other positions of responsibility. He was named rector of the Cathedral of Morelia, then apostolic administrator in the Diocese of Chilapa. As a capable and trusted pastor, Martinez was ordained auxiliary bishop and vicar general of Morelia in 1923. He held this post until 1937, when he was named primate archbishop of Mexico City.

Father Pedro Fernandez, O.P., the biographer of Archbishop Martinez and the postulator for his cause of beatification, described four distinct periods characterizing the productive life and ministry of Luis Maria Martinez: *his years in the seminary, his social apostolate, his work as spiritual director, and his years as bishop.*

As *director of the seminary*, Martinez's principal concerns were the academic, disciplinary, and spiritual renewal of the seminary and the seminarians. This stage of growth came to a violent end in July 1914, when revolutionary troops opposing the Church destroyed the seminary library with its precious collection of more than fifty thousand volumes, and vandalized the building. Undaunted, Martinez carried on, training the reduced number of students who were forced to live in private residences until the political situation improved.

Martinez responded to these turbulent times of Church persecution in Mexico with a *social apostolate*. This consisted of forming a group of Catholic lay leaders to be actively involved in society and politics. His goal was for these lay leaders to establish a Catholic government in order to change the pervading atheistic and unjust laws into laws that would respect religion and the human person. Martinez never supported violence or taking up arms. Instead, he always sought the good of his country and tried to maintain balance between the enemies of the Church and the general population, most of whom were Catholics.

It is easy to understand why Martinez, a man of deep spirituality, would be a sought-after *spiritual director* for priests, men and women religious, and lay people. He contributed his greatest and most polished writings to the field of spirituality.

Finally, *as a bishop*, Martinez was entirely dedicated to his pastoral ministry. A holy and devoted servant of God, he dedicated himself to the care of his priests and the spiritual development of his people, to teaching and guiding, to prudently seeking peaceful resolutions to the persecution of the Church, and above all, to fostering his own spiritual life, which led him to great heights of holiness. At his death, as a poor archbishop without material possessions, he was considered rich in spiritual gifts to the point that the people exclaimed: "A saint has died."

What does my heart long for? What does God's Spirit yearn for in my regard?

We are people of restless hearts, living in a busy age, surrounded by a cacophony of noises that bombard us all day long. Often we dart through this loud, speeding world trying to find something or someone that can satisfy the deep longing at the center of our being. That which is good, true, and beautiful in our world can certainly make us happy. But at some point our hearts need further reassurance, because there is a deep space within each of us that cannot be filled by finite matter, things, or people. It can only be filled by God.

Many people don't even recognize this inner yearning because of its many guises: boredom, dissatisfaction, crises, and desires we can never satisfy. We seek more money, relationships, sex, substances, activities, honors, entertainment, and distractions. But these things can only satisfy our longing temporarily.

Some people turn to today's popular wisdom writers to find clever ways of naming and explaining humanity's yearning. Television personalities and evangelists promote attractive messages to those who are searching. Books, blogs, videos, the internet, and social networking sites pick up the same ideas, and before long popular movements spring up. People sincerely search for spiritual answers. But secular prophets, although well intentioned and sincere, offer only partial answers. Many movements remain on a natural level, devoid of reference to God. Perhaps they identify a being, force, universe, or wisdom figure that stands for something and someone greater than themselves. But that is not enough. Attempts to understand suffering prove inadequate. Every effort is made to help people avoid all pain and always be happy. Yet, evading suffering and pain proves to be impossible.

We can only find satisfactory and lasting answers to the problem of evil and suffering when we discover a personal God who loves us and redeems us through Jesus Christ his Son. Only the biblical God can bring us peace and happiness, because this God is not an abstract concept, but a *person* who longs for union and communion with us. Only this God of Love can fill our hearts with the joy and peace for which we long. Martinez understood this truth, lived it throughout his life, and expressed it in his writings with clarity and beauty.

The God who is Love pursues and woos us. In his immense affection for us, he sent his Son, Jesus Christ, who, through the mystery of *kenosis* or self-emptying, became one of us and saved us through his life, suffering, death, and resurrection.

Since our earthly journey inevitably comes face to face with the cross, we turn to Jesus who made suffering sacred by taking it upon himself, and we learn from him. He did not hold back, but gave us the gift of himself, his total love.

Martinez highlights the hope-filled message of God's love and concern, and speaks of the Holy Spirit as the sweet companion of our souls. He describes well the human struggle to grow in union with Jesus as we seek to develop our interior life. Never glossing over the reality of sin and suffering, Martinez offers the hopeful message that "the work, pain, and sufferings of this world do not constitute the definitive atmosphere of our souls. Our atmosphere is rest in God."[1]

"I have a special place in the thought of God," writes Archbishop Luis Maria Martinez. "I occupy a post of honor in his heart; I am the unique object of his providence and his action. . . . My life, with its alternations of joy and grief, fear and hope, activity and repose; my life, with its variable and innumerable circumstances, is God's work. It is the fruit of his love."[2]

I

God's Gift of Peace

Peace is the gift that Jesus Christ brought us from heaven, his gift, the gift of God. It is a gift so beautiful, so profound, so all-embracing, and efficacious, that we shall never truly comprehend it.

We might say concerning peace what our Lord said of himself to the Samaritan woman at Jacob's well: "If you knew the gift of God . . ." (Jn 4:10). Truly, if we understood this God-given gift of peace, we could appreciate how it is the synthesis, the very peak, so to speak, of all the graces and heavenly blessings we have received in Christ Jesus.

Peace is the seal of Christ. It is not just one of his many gifts; it is, in a certain way, his own gift. When Jesus appeared in the world on that unforgettable night in Bethlehem, the angels proclaimed peace. On another unforgettable night, the last that he spent on earth, the pivotal night of the Cenacle and the Eucharist, Jesus left peace to his loved ones as a testament of his love: "Peace I leave with you; my peace I give to you" (Jn 14:27).

Our Lord's customary greeting to his apostles after his resurrection was "Peace be with you!" Furthermore, he recommended that in pursuing their apostolic mission, they should always say these words upon arriving at any house: "Peace be with you" (Jn 20:21, 26), and any person of peace who dwelt there should receive their peace; if not, their good wishes for peace should return to the apostles. . . .

 Our Lord's peace has distinctive characteristics, which call for at least a brief consideration. First, it is a peace *exclusively his own*; he has a monopoly on peace. On the eve of his passion, he said to his disciples: "Peace I leave with you; my peace I give to you. I do not give to you as the world gives" (Jn 14:27).

The world, which counterfeits everything, cannot counterfeit peace, no matter how much it tries. It misrepresents joy; the world's happiness is always superficial and sometimes even bitter. The world counterfeits wisdom, dazzling the credulous with a showy but empty knowledge. It counterfeits love, giving this sacred name to mere passion or to base egoism. The world, the offspring of Satan, father of lies, is essentially an imposter, falsifying everything. But it is powerless in counterfeiting one thing: peace. The world cannot give peace because peace is a divine thing; it is the seal of Jesus Christ.

A second characteristic of our Lord's peace is its *profundity*. It is not superficial, merely exterior, the peace of the tomb or the desert. Such is not really peace, but solitude, emptiness, desolation. The peace of God, on the other hand, reaches even to the depths of our hearts. It pervades our innermost being, penetrating it like an exquisite perfume. Peace is plenitude; it is life.

Thirdly, peace is *indestructible*. Nothing and no one can force the peace of heaven out of a person who has received this gift of God. Neither the persecutions of tyrants, nor the snares of the devil, nor the vicissitudes of earth can disturb a soul in which God has established his peace.

On the night before his passion, Jesus told his apostles that he gave them his joy and added: ". . . and no one will take your joy from you" (Jn 16:22). The same may be said of peace: "Nobody can take it away from you." Everything else may be taken away from us: our homes, property, liberty, and even our lives. In a certain sense, we can be deprived of happiness. It is true that perfect joy can be experienced even when the eyes weep and the heart suffers, but such heights are characteristic of only very elevated, perfect souls. Consequently enemies may take from us, in some measure, even our joy. But they can never deprive us of peace when Jesus has given it to us. Peace can continue its reign in our hearts in spite of the miseries, sadness, and bitterness of life.

Finally, the peace of Christ is a *rich* peace, full of sweetness and mildness. Saint Paul describes it as "the peace of God, which surpasses all understanding" (Phil 4:7). This peace is the only form of happiness unparalleled upon earth; it is the substance of heaven. Without the splendors of the beatific vision, without the overflowing happiness of that everlasting state, peace is the substance of what we hope to enjoy in heaven. . . .

But is it always possible to preserve peace of soul? Should our hearts never be disturbed by anything at all? . . . I would like to present the means whereby the soul may preserve peace despite all obstacles.

The first path to peace is faith. In fact, if we lived by faith, we would live in peace. . . .

Faith teaches that God loves us, and that he loves us not as a group, but personally, individually. "He loved *me!*" (cf. Gal 2:20). Each one of us can make these words of Saint Paul our own without fear of error. God knows my name; he has engraved my image in his heart. Still more, I can be assured that his heart is all mine because our Lord cannot love as we do, by halves. When he loves, he loves with his whole heart, infinitely. . . .

We may go a step farther. God's love for us is not a sterile love, confined to heaven. It is an active love, provident, watchful, solicitous. It is a love that does not forget us for one moment, but protects us unceasingly, and keeps arranging minutely all the events of our life from the most far-reaching to the most insignificant.

I am not exaggerating. Jesus himself affirmed it: "But not a hair of your head will perish" (Lk 21:18). Some persons may consider this hyperbole. Perhaps, but at any rate it is a hyperbole that expresses the solicitude, constancy, and minute care of God's love for us. . . .

Through what strange phenomenon, through what inexplicable illusion do we Christians disquiet ourselves, knowing with the certainty of faith that a loving God bears us in his arms and surrounds us with his divine tenderness?

— Excerpts from *Only Jesus*, pp. 13–19

II

The Language of Silence

Silence, even naturally speaking, invites us to concentrate and think about serious, profound things. For example, when we are in the midst of a forest, or on the ocean, or in a deserted place, we feel the need to concentrate and recollect ourselves. Due to our psychological structure, noise forces us outside of ourselves, distracting us and scattering our powers. It forces our spirit to skip around through external things. But when silence prevails, we can again concentrate and live within.

In accordance with this law of our psychology, we need to live within to live with God, because we always find God in the interior of our soul. It is natural that exterior silence is not only an invitation to an interior life, but a necessary condition for that life of intimate communication with God. The atmosphere of the interior life, of the contemplative life, is silence. Hence, the masters of the spiritual life recommend it so highly. . . .

In order to live the contemplative life, or the religious life in any of its forms, exterior silence is indispensable. This is true for all true interior life. We must realize its importance in living above and not below, in living a life of intimacy and union with God. Let us not forget that silence should not be treated as a mere constraint or as a means of order like those used in a school or in a class, but as a necessary condition for living within and not living without. . . .

The contemplative life is an intimate affair. It is a loving conversation of a person with God. But in order that God may speak to the soul, and the soul speak with God, silence is necessary. Neither God nor our hearts will be silent, but the earth and created things must be hushed because everything worldly hinders the intimate conversation of our souls with God.

This silence is not the silence of the desert nor of the tomb—a negative silence, the lack or suspension of life. It is like the apparel of a more interior life that one wears outside because inside he is singing a love song. He does not speak with creatures, because he is speaking with God; he does not listen to the noise of earth, so that he may hear the harmonies of heaven.

As an audience maintains silence to hear better the voice of an orator, as music lovers keep silence during a symphony to admire its artistic beauty, so the silence of contemplation is nothing other than the indispensable condition for hearing the voice of God and speaking to him with heartfelt words. . . .

. . . [W]hen we see a splendid spectacle of nature, we are silent. Ordinary sights, on the contrary, make us talk and we casually comment on them. But we fall silent before something sublime. Therefore, admiration, sorrow, love, all the great sentiments of our heart, all the deep impressions of our soul are like this: when imperfect and limited they can be expressed with human speech. But when they increase and reach their peak, they cannot be expressed by weak words. Their only language is silence.

In heaven, love is not expressed in this way because another language exists there, a language not of this earth. Here below the greatest love is silent love. Such is the love of Jesus in the Eucharist.

Happy are we if we love Jesus with that sublime silence! Many a time our love speaks, our love sings, our love expresses itself in various ways. But when love increases in our hearts, it tends to become silent. That is when it has reached maturity. It has become so intense and so deep that it cannot be expressed with our dull human language.

— Excerpts from Only Jesus, pp. 38–40, 55

III

Confidence in God

B e as delicate as you can with our Lord. Watch your conduct most carefully to avoid all venial sins. But, for the love of God, do this without losing confidence and peace.

I recommend this counsel to such a degree that, if it were necessary to lose these two goods, confidence and peace, in order to arrive at this exquisite delicacy, I maintain that it would be preferable to restrain one's efforts for a while. For peace of soul and confidence in God are more necessary goods, so they should be preferred. . . .

No doubt someone will say: How is it possible to feel that keen grief for one's offense against God, yet have the confidence necessary to cast oneself into the arms of our Lord, without any misgivings or reserve? I will try to explain.

The foundation of our confidence does not rest in us, but in God. Hence we trust in our Lord and we draw near to him, tranquil and sure, not because of what we are, but because of what he is. We can be miserable sinners, wayward and headstrong. But our ingratitude, our sins, and our wrongdoing should not diminish at all the trust that we should have in our Lord, for the simple reason that our trust is not based in ourselves but in him. Jesus is the same forever, ever good, ever loving, ever merciful. I was the one who changed, but these changes in no way affect my confidence, since my confidence is based on God, not on myself. . . .

We have confidence in God because of his goodness, mercy, and love. And does God cease to be good and merciful because I am weak, inconstant, and miserable? Impossible! . . . We are trying to judge God in a human manner. We would measure his divine heart with the yardstick of our petty heart, and it is not God's yardstick. We, of course, conduct ourselves with everyone according to his merits. We are good toward those who treat us well, and we are indifferent toward strangers. Only virtue can keep us from being hostile toward our enemies. In order that our hearts may love, they must always take into account those which reside in others. For our love has its basis in the things that we love—in the goodness that they possess, or seem to possess. But that is not the basis of God's love. The measure and the reason of his love does not reside in things or in us; they are in him and in him alone. . . .

I maintain that if an angel should come from God to tell any of us, "God no longer loves you; hence do not confide in him," we must not believe him. For above this feigned revelation stands the words of Jesus, "Heaven and earth will pass away, but my words will not pass away" (Mk 13:31). Jesus is the one who brought us a message from heaven. He came to tell us that God loves us with an infinite love, with an eternal love. He loves us to the extent of giving us his own Son, and delivering him to death for love of us.

— Excerpts from *Secrets of the Interior Life*, pp. 34–39, 41

IV

God's Gentleness and Mildness

Who would find it easy to believe that to become a saint, mildness is just as necessary as strength, perhaps even more so? Mildness is not weakness; rather it indicates strength. Weak souls do their works with noise and show; the strong operate with marvelous gentleness. Life is as strong as it is gentle, while love is as powerful as it is delicate. So the action of God upon nature, in history, and on souls is infinitely mighty and infinitely mild.

The action of God upon his saints is most gentle. How he respects our freedom! How he condescends to our weakness! He does not run, jump, or act violently. We rush, being weak creatures, but God works slowly because he deals with eternity. We bewail the passage of minutes, but God serenely watches the flow of years. We wish to achieve the goal of our desires in a hurry, but God prepares his work gently. Our inconstancy does not tire him, nor do our failures startle him, nor do the complicated vicissitudes of human life overturn his eternal designs.

Conversions are prodigies of gentleness, as Saint Augustine's was. The long stages necessary for union are prodigies of gentleness, as were the paths Saint Theresa traveled. Great missions from God are also prodigies of gentleness, as Saint Margaret Mary Alacoque's was. If we knew how to study the divine action in every saint, in every soul, we would be astonished, perhaps more at the gentleness than at the power of the sanctifying action.

Gentleness is indispensable for us if we are to become holy, something we often forget. Undoubtedly many souls do not sanctify themselves because of a lack of power; but many also, indeed very many, fail to do so because of a lack of gentleness.

The human soul is precious and delicate. It came forth from the divine lips as a most gentle breath. The divine blood of Jesus cleanses it and renders it beautiful. And the soul is destined to be united with God himself and to participate in the life and ineffable mystery of the most Blessed Trinity.

Such an exquisite jewel must be handled with great delicacy. That is how God treats it, and that is how we should treat it. What an atmosphere of purity of mind, of peace, and of delicacy ought to surround a soul for it to achieve its sanctification! When the soul is borne to another atmosphere, it pines and laments! It is like those beautiful and delicate flowers that a strong wind withers or the heat of the sun discolors and parches.

I think that the greater part of the spiritual ills of those who seek perfection comes from a lack of gentleness. Our poor, ever disquieted souls need gentleness. Desiring holiness, they want to achieve it all at once. They cannot bear their own miseries. They grow angry at their weaknesses, and with an over-refinement of ingenuity they continually worry and grieve themselves. . . .

Mildness is necessary to those who are strict with themselves to the point of excess. They have forgotten the pages of the Gospel, which tell us about mercy and love. They see in Christ only the severe face of a Judge, without remembering that he is also our Friend, Father, Spouse, and above all, Savior who came to heal our miseries. They do not know that the sweet honey of love achieves more with the poor human heart than the bitter gall of severity.

— Excerpts from *Secrets of the Interior Life*, pp. 54–57

V

Love, Sorrow, Fruitfulness

One of the most important things in the spiritual life is to understand well the close relationship between love and sacrifice. It is easily understood that love is the basis of perfection, and the soul delights in confirming it. For love marvelously corresponds to something deep that the soul bears in its interior: a vital yearning that is vehement and, in a certain sense, unparalleled. And when we come in contact with what is fleeting and superficial, the emptiness of the affections of earth, we impetuously fling toward divine love. That love is so profound that it reaches to the deepest part of our soul, into regions that mundane affections never touch. It is so perfect that it satisfies forever without ever tiring. It is so enduring that it is immortal and so abiding that nothing and no one can uproot it when it has implanted itself in our heart.

Frequently, however, one has an inexact concept of love. . . . It [the soul] does not understand that in this life, to love is to suffer, that on this earth, the eternal symbol of love is the cross of Christ. . . .

When we come to understand that perfection consists in love, and that this love is attained, conserved, and consummated only by sacrifice, then we have found the path of sanctity, for then we have entered the luminous region of truth. . . .

Love snatches the soul from all things, even from itself, and places it in ineffable and magnificent solitude. . . . Ordinarily we do not take account of the solitariness that love causes in our hearts except when separation or death deprives us of that beloved object upon whom love centers our lives and our beings, after isolating us from all other things. Who has not felt this? The world has not changed. Life follows its course, the sky remains blue, flowers diffuse their perfumes, birds sing, the sun warms and gives life, the same things surround us and the same people associate with us. But alas, one thing is absent, one thing alone. It is enough to make us feel lonely in the midst of a multitude, to induce a vast void in the soul, to make the earth appear to us like a desert. . . .

. . . [T]here is no comparison between the solitariness produced by human love and that which divine love demands, for there is no comparison between these two loves. Human love is shallow, divine love is profound. The first is partial and fragmentary; it never completely embraces the heart. The second is entire, absorbing, unparalleled. Human love has its own tint, and excludes at least all affections of that shade, but divine love embraces all colors, and consequently it excludes all other loves.

. . . [W]hat can I give to God, if he is in himself eternally rich, happy, the fount of love, and ocean of beatitude? What can I give him, if I receive everything from him?

Lord, I feel the compelling need to love you. It is my duty, my glory, my happiness. If I do not love you, my life has no reason for being. O God of love! If love consists in giving, how can I love you? And if I cannot love you, how can I live?

There is one thing I can give to God, only one; I can give him glory. The universe was created for the glory of God. Christ lived and the Church exists for the glory of God. I ought to live for the glory of God. To love God is to give him glory. The motto of Saint Ignatius, "For the greater glory of God," is the supreme formula of love. . . .

When I give glory to God, I do a divine work. My action has the same end as the action of God. I rise above all created things. I enter into the thoughts and desires of God. If it were known what the glory of God is, one would think of nothing else. One would love that glory as the saints have loved it, passionately, regarding as lost every action that did not have it as its purpose. . . .

Heaven is the country of love, yet on earth one can burn with seraphic love. With Jesus and love, everywhere is heaven. There is one difference between the heaven of time and the heaven of eternity. No one will suffer in the latter. Here, suffering abounds. Does not this difference give a certain advantage to the earthly heaven? Is the value of suffering understood? Is its excellence esteemed? Is its beauty known? The only thing that the angels would envy us, if they were capable of envy, would be suffering. God fell in love with this precious pearl hidden among life's miseries. He loved it, came and died from it. The angels cannot say to God: "I love you even to sacrifice, even to death." Only human beings can taste the delicacy of that phrase.

— Excerpts from *Secrets of the Interior Life*, pp. 59–62;
Only Jesus, pp. 97–99, 101

VI

Our Hidden God

You fill the universe with your majesty, history with your thought and action, souls with your presence, and the Church with your word and Eucharist. You are present everywhere and in innumerable ways. You surround, envelop, and penetrate us. In you we live and move and have our being (cf. Acts 17:28). Nevertheless, the greater part of the human race forgets you. Many people offend you, while many do not know you, and many deny you. Truly you are a God of hidden ways, everywhere present and everywhere hidden. . . .

Even in heaven, your supreme and glorious Epiphany [manifestation], you are a hidden God, not indeed for the angels who praise you, nor for those who enjoy you, but for us who wander through the desert of this world longing for you, seeking you in the dimness of holy hope. O God, ever present and ever hidden! Blessed are the souls who seek you. More blessed are those who find you and enjoy you in the secrecy of your benign presence.

But I feel the necessity of meditating upon something that concerns me so intimately. I am not a creature like the other creatures of the earth, since God placed in me a soul, the breath of his mouth—a soul purchased with the blood of Christ and beautified with the gifts of the Holy Spirit. I have a special place in the thought of God. I occupy a post of honor in his heart. I am the unique object of his providence and his action. God is singularly present in my life and in my soul. God is for me a God present and hidden. Not for a single instant does the action of God fail to touch me—not only his power that preserves and moves all creatures, but more especially, his exceedingly gentle action that keeps guiding me along unknown paths toward my perfection and happiness.

I do not understand how much God loves me nor how immense, constant, and active is the love he has for me. Not for one instant does he fail to draw me toward himself with the force of his love of predilection. My life is God's work, my life with its alternations of joy and grief, fear and hope, activity and rest, and with all its variable and innumerable circumstances. It is the fruit of his love. God foresees everything in my life, and he directs and disposes of it for my good. Only when I separate myself from him by sin does my life cease to be the fruit of his action. Yet God permits even my faults, then returns to convert me and to repair the damage caused by sin.

Beneath all external happenings, God is always present and hidden. Joy and sorrow are equally God's messengers coming to accomplish in my soul the work of his love. They are instruments of his action, veils that cover his presence. If only I would continue to discover this God hidden in my own life! If I would always let myself be led by his gentle hand, my life would be his action, my soul, a temple, and I, a saint.

— Excerpts from *Only Jesus*, pp. 68, 70–71

VII

Reproducing Jesus in Us

If we are hidden in Christ, we are united to him. What a consoling thought! Can it be true? United to Christ, who is light, peace, love, felicity—all! That is to be in heaven. United through faith, hope, charity, united through the Eucharist. When fear overwhelms us, let us strengthen our union with him. Let us embrace him as children embrace their mothers when they foresee danger. Let us hide ourselves in him. It is so sweet to rest in the heart of Christ. And even when we do not experience fear, let us unite ourselves to him. Our very life is union with him. For us to live is to be hidden in Christ: "For to me, living is

Christ and dying is gain" (Phil 1:21). "[Y]our life is hidden with Christ in God" (Col 3:3). The atmosphere which our souls breathe is Christ; the blood that vivifies us is Christ; the bread that nourishes us is Christ; the wine that stimulates us is Christ; our life is, in a word, Christ.

Let us breathe, let us eat, let us drink, let us live Christ!

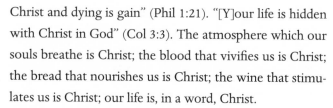

Christian life is the reproduction of Jesus in us. Perfection, the most faithful and perfect reproduction, consists in our transformation into Jesus. This is the teaching of Saint Paul, set forth time and again in his letters: "Do you not realize that Jesus Christ is in you?" (2 Cor 13:5). "As many of you as were baptized into Christ have clothed yourselves with Christ" (Gal 3:27). "[A]nd that Christ may dwell in your hearts through faith" (Eph 3:17). "For those whom he foreknew he also predestined to be conformed to the image of his Son" (Rom 8:29). These verses are among the many expressions of the Apostle relative to Christian life.

As for perfection, these profoundly comprehensive words are well known: "[I]t is no longer I who live, but it is Christ who lives in me" (Gal 2:20). The word "transformation" is also from Saint Paul: "And all of us, with unveiled faces, seeing the glory of the Lord as though reflected in a mirror, are being transformed into the same image from one degree of glory to another" (2 Cor 3:18).

— Excerpts from *Only Jesus*, pp. 110–111;
The Sanctifier, pp. 5–6

VIII

With Our Whole Heart

Whenever the affections of the heart are not an expansion of divine love, they are an obstacle to our perfect union with God.

Every affection, to be sure, is not an obstacle, for when divine love takes possession of a soul, it enriches the soul with most pure loves. Since these spring from the sturdy trunk of the love of God, they are far from being an obstacle. They are, rather, a powerful help to the most intimate union, to perfect holiness, since they are expansions of divine love.

From its inception, the love of God demands of us that we love our neighbor, that is to say, all people, good and bad, friends and enemies. And in the exuberance of charity the saints come to love not only the neighbor, whom they are obliged to love, but even inanimate creatures. Saint Francis of Assisi is a magnificent example of this spiritual exuberance of love. His heart embraced with the immense sweep of love, not only human beings, but also all creation: the sun, water, fish, birds, and even the wolf. . . .

. . . [O]ur Lord taught us in so clear and so precise a manner that, if we are to achieve perfection, an absolute renunciation of all things of this world is necessary. We must root out from our hearts everything that is not the love of God or that does not have its origin in this love. This is the truth he set as the foundation of his doctrine in his sermon on the beatitudes: "Blessed are the poor in spirit, for theirs is the kingdom of heaven" (Mt 5:3). The kingdom of heaven is union with God. It is all-consuming love; it is full participation in the life of God. And the kingdom of God is for the poor, for those who renounce themselves, for those who have sold all that they possessed, for those who find themselves in the holy and divine nakedness of poverty and of love. . . .

For it is impossible to reach holiness without renouncing our possessions, without freeing our hearts of them. God will not take full possession of our hearts until they have been freed of everything else. As long as the root of the last disorderly affection that abides in us is not pulled out, the love of God cannot reign with full sovereignty. . . .

Considered from the heart of Jesus, disorderly affections are enemies of love. Each of them robs Jesus of a fiber of our heart. And he desires that we love him with our whole heart. In fact, this demand of our Lord is most just. For how could we reasonably share it, seeing that it is so poor and so small? . . .

If we love, let us give our whole heart. Let us not concern ourselves too much about our frailties and our failings. Nobody knows better than Jesus the clay from which we are formed. Nobody knows better than he how to commiserate with our weakness and how to condescend to our frailty. The one thing we should concern ourselves with is our heart. Let it be pure and free of all attachments; let it be solely for Jesus. Let us not hold back the least fragment of our heart. Let us not take the minutest particle for ourselves: all must be for Jesus.

— Excerpts from *Secrets of the Interior Life*, pp. 17–18, 20–22, 28, 30

IX

Resting in God's Heart

The holy Gospel relates that after the apostles first went out on their apostolic mission, Jesus said to them: "Come away to a deserted place all by yourselves and rest a while" (Mk 6:31). The Gospel tells us nothing of how they took that rest, but we can easily conjecture what peace, love, and happiness that secret, intimate retreat with Jesus must have held for them.

On some occasions in life, God approaches the soul and speaks similar words, inviting it with immense tenderness to rest sweetly within his divine heart and—dare I say it?—asking it to allow him to rest in it.

Heaven is complete rest in God, because earth is always a place of labor, vicissitudes, and sorrow. The soul sighs to be freed from the anxieties of this life, as Saint Paul desired: ". . . [M]y desire is to depart and be with Christ" (Phil 1:23). But God, the divine friend, is pleased to grant to souls that love him an experience of beatitude on this earth, in the heaven of his heart—is not that incomparable heart a heaven?—by inviting them to the repose of purity, love, and peace within himself.

Our poor heart longs for that rest because we are born for heaven. The work, pain, and sufferings of this world do not constitute the definitive atmosphere of our soul. Our atmosphere is rest in God and it is formed by those divine elements of which I have spoken: light, purity, love, and peace.

The divine oasis of the Sacred Heart, that secret and entrancing heaven, is opened up to the chosen soul who will find an indescribable repose within it. Let the soul hasten to cast its cares and worries into the flames of Christ's heart, to be totally consumed. Trustful and happy, let it enter into the place of repose to dwell in holy abundance, transported with life and with love. At the same time, the individual must forget earthly things in order to be content with Jesus only, to bask in the splendor of the heart that loves so much, and to be filled with the holy fire, the heavenly tenderness and the immortal life enclosed in that divine vessel.

The soul that would rest in God must dwell in self-forgetfulness and surrender. The forgetfulness of love! The surrender of love! Is it not love, possibly, that is forgotten and abandoned? In order to love, one must forget everything and center one's gaze, heart, and life upon the Beloved.

The heart of Jesus is an unfathomable abyss of love. "God is love," said Saint John (1 Jn 4:16). Blessed Angela of Foligno relates that on one occasion God said to her: "Look at me well. Is there anything in me that is not love?" All in him is love, an inexhaustible, unique, eternal love. On account of our slight experience with love, we see only faintly that it is noble and heavenly, that it fulfills our aspirations and seals our happiness. But on earth love is limited because mere creatures cannot contain the infinite. If we wish to drink that heavenly draught in human hearts, sooner or later we drain all that earth's fragile, limited chalices contain of it. Our thirst is never satisfied, because our capacity and our desires are infinite—our only infinite possession. The only fountain of love that is never exhausted is God, and that fountain is in the divine heart of Jesus. We can drink eternally from it without ever emptying it, because our soul's capacity makes our thirst for love infinite. The fountain of love in Jesus's heart is infinite, because it springs from the divine fullness. "Open your mouth wide and I will fill it," says the Scripture (Ps 81:10). Open your mouth, the mouth of desire with which you drink love; open it wide and I shall fill it. Blessed are the souls who dwell in the interior of Jesus's heart! They will always drink from that sweet fountain without ever exhausting it.

An inexhaustible love! Who understands this mystery of happiness? Everything on earth runs out: joy and sorrow, fecundity and life itself. All created things, however beautiful, however perfect, have a limit, a measure, an end. We are so accustomed to finish things and use them up that we do not comprehend the mystery of an inexhaustible love. In its endless desire for love, our heart glimpses infinite love as one dimly glimpses the vast firmament when the spirit wanders from star to star in the immensity of the night.

— Excerpts from *Only Jesus*, pp. 219–220, 179–180

X

The Holy Spirit, Delightful Guest

How wonderful is the work of the artist! By efforts both ardent and gentle he can infuse hard and shapeless materials with the light of his soul. The instruments he uses, though often crude, can impart to these materials exquisite proportions and shapes.

That is the way one may conceive the sanctifying work of the Holy Spirit, Artist of souls. Is not sanctity the supreme art? God has only one ideal, which, in its prodigious unity and because it is divine, encompasses all the highest forms of beauty. This ideal is Jesus. The Holy Spirit loves him more than an artist loves his ideal. That love is his being, because the Holy Spirit is nothing but love, the personal Love of the Father and of the Word.[3] With divine enthusiasm he comes to the soul—the soul, breath of the Most High, spiritual light that can be united with uncreated Light, exquisite essence that can be transformed into Jesus, reproducing the eternal idea.

That which the human artist dreams of without ever being able to attain, the divine Artist accomplishes because he is perfect and infinite. His action is not exterior nor intermittent, but intimate and constant. He enters into the depths of our souls, penetrates the innermost recesses, and takes up his permanent dwelling there to produce later on his magnificent work. . . .

. . . [T]he first relationship that the Holy Spirit has with us is that of being the delightful Guest—*dulcis Hospes animae*—as the Church calls him in the inspired prose of the Mass of Pentecost. Without doubt, the entire Blessed Trinity dwells within the soul living the life of grace, as it is to dwell eternally within the soul living the life of glory—the full and joyous expansion of the life of grace. . . .

Without this dwelling of the Holy Spirit in us we cannot "become Christ." "Anyone who does not have the Spirit of Christ does not belong to him" (Rom 8:9). Grace and charity, which are the life of our souls, have relationship with the Spirit who dwells in us, because "God's love has been poured into our hearts through the Holy Spirit that has been given to us" (Rom 5:5). . . .

And the Holy Spirit does not come to us in a transitory manner. Infinite Love is not a passing visitor who pays us a call and then goes away. He establishes in us his permanent dwelling and lives in intimate union with our souls as their eternal Guest. Jesus promised this to us on the last night of his mortal life: "And I will ask the Father, and he will give you another Advocate, to be with you forever. This is the Spirit of truth, whom the world cannot receive, because it neither sees him nor knows him. You know him, because he abides with you, and he will be in you" (Jn 14:16–17).

— Excerpts from *The Sanctifier*, pp. 9–11

XI

The Holy Spirit and the Virtues

When God wishes to fill a heart with his greatness, all that is created must go out of it. This emptiness is demanded by the Holy Spirit, who aspires to fullness of possession; it is required by the holy exigencies of a "love . . . strong as death" (Song 8:6), which separates and mercilessly roots out everything else from the soul and leaves the profound and delightful solitude of union.

But if love separates, it is in order to unite. If it roots out, it is in order to plant. If it empties, it is to fill; if it puts the soul in solitude, it is to bring plenitude. Those who love should be left alone to look at each other without interference, to love without disturbance, to speak without witnesses, to pour out their hearts in isolation, in the most pure and intimate union.

The delightful Guest of our soul aspires to this union, and the mystery of it is accomplished by the theological virtues. . . .

. . . [The] loving intimacy that the Spirit longs for, the soul sighs for, cannot be brought about except by the theological virtues. To repeat: the other virtues empty the soul, place it in the desired solitude, cleanse and adorn it. But for communicating with the Beloved in this solitude, the theological virtues are necessary. The eyes of *faith* contemplate him among the shadows. The arms of *hope* reach him beyond time in the triumph of eternity. The heart of *charity* loves him with a created love made to the image and likeness of love uncreated. This is the bond that ties the soul close to the Holy Spirit; this is the essence of all perfection and the form of all virtue.

Faith

The presence of the Holy Spirit in our souls demands that we know, that we have the firm conviction of his indwelling, of our living under his very glance, of his seeking our own glance. How sweet to live in the light of that mutual glance!—a light so penetrating at times that it seems to plunge into the bosom of God, so bright that it resembles the dawn of the eternal day, so gentle that it seems to radiate from heaven. Then life is easy and pleasant in the depths of the soul, in loving intimacy with the divine Guest.

At times, however, the soul's heaven grows dark, and in the great stretches of solitude the person cannot find a single ray of light or a vestige of the former delight. It seems that the heart is empty, that the soul has lost its priceless treasure. How difficult it is to be recollected. At such times the hours pass with tedium, and with what bitterness the soul drags itself along the path that leads to God! But in the midst of these necessary difficulties of the spiritual life, there is something that does not change nor end, something very solid that does not permit the soul to get lost, and which, like a sure compass, marks out its divine course. It is faith that always reveals the divine to us wherever it is. It is faith that makes us look at the delightful Guest, both in the shadows of desolation and in the full, heavenly brilliance of consolation.

The Scriptures tell us that "The one who is righteous will live by faith" (Rom 1:17). For this reason Saint John of the Cross recommends so emphatically, for souls aspiring to union with God, this life of faith as the straight and sure path to the summit.

Our devotion to the Holy Spirit, then, must be founded on faith. It is the basis of the Christian life. It accomplishes our first communication with God, and it initiates our intimacy with the Holy Spirit, producing in our soul that glance which unites us with the Spirit of Light called by the Church "Most blessed Light! Most happy Light!"

Hope

Through the theological virtue of hope we tend toward God, our end, our good, our happiness. And we tend toward him not with the uncertainty and inconstancy of human hope, but with the unshakable support of his loving strength. The goal of our hope is in the heavenly fatherland, for there we shall have eternal and full possession of God. We have the divine promise that cannot deceive: heaven and earth shall pass away but not the word of God (cf. Mt 24:35). And if, together with hope, we have charity in our souls, we have more than the promise: we possess in substance the good that we shall possess fully in heaven. The Holy Spirit, our Guest, our Gift, is the pledge of our inheritance. As Saint Paul says: "In him you also, when you had heard the word of truth, the gospel of your salvation, and had believed in him, were marked with the seal of the promised Holy Spirit; this is the pledge of our inheritance" (Eph 1:13–14). . . .

To understand the practical importance of the virtue of hope, let us note the most common and most dangerous obstacle in the way of perfection: discouragement. This results from the faults, temptations, and aridity found in every spiritual life. It reduces fervor and generosity and impedes progress to perfection. While we have confidence, any obstacle can be overcome, any sacrifice is easily made, and our struggles are crowned with victory. But when discouragement invades the soul, it is left without energy or support and thus is easily deterred, misguided, and confused. . . .

The more we advance in the spiritual life, the stronger must be our hope. For the struggles become more terrible, the sacrifices greater, and the intimate operations of grace more profound and more difficult to understand. . . . Hope is a supernatural capacity for receiving the Holy Spirit who aids and sanctifies, with all the divine streams that spring from this fountain. When he himself has satisfied the thirst of our souls, our hope is fulfilled, because he is the Spirit of the promise and the pledge of our inheritance, as we have heard from the lips of Saint Paul.

Love

What we have said about detachment and loving attention to the Guest of our souls and about the exercise of faith and hope has only been a preparation for that which constitutes the foundation of devotion to the Holy Spirit: namely, love. Love is essential in this devotion because the Holy Spirit is the infinite and personal Love of God. His work is a work of love. What he seeks and longs for is to establish the reign of love. How can we meet love except with love? How can we fulfill its desires and satisfy its divine requirements, cooperate with its plans, and utilize its gifts, except by love?

The most perfect and excellent love is that of charity. The divine Spirit pours into our hearts the third theological virtue, that we may have this love. Saint Paul composed a magnificent tribute to the virtue of charity in the First Letter to the Corinthians (chapter 13). There he shows that charity is the most excellent of the gifts of God, the form of all the virtues, something divine and heavenly that does not end with life but accompanies the soul into eternity.

Charity is the most perfect image of the Holy Spirit, with whom it has a very close relationship. When charity is in the soul, the Holy Spirit lives in it, and when the Spirit gives himself to a soul, he pours charity into it. The degree of charity in any soul is the measure of the mutual possession that exists between itself and the Spirit. It is the measure of all the infused virtues and of the gifts of the Spirit. It is the measure of grace and of glory. . . .

The exercise of charity is a brief and delightful road for attaining sanctity. It is brief, because everything is simplified when it is treated thoroughly. It is delightful, because love facilitates every effort, and devotion every sacrifice. How easy is the way when one loves! How courageous, how strong, and how filled with consolation is the soul that is sustained by love!

— Excerpts from *The Sanctifier*, pp. 61, 63–65, 67–73

XII

A Deep Interior Life

Nothing is more important in the supernatural order than to have a deep, intense interior life. At times we run into the error of subordinating the interior life to the practice of the virtues, as if our contact with God were only a means to perfect ourselves.

That is not so. Certainly prayer and all the other acts of the interior life have an efficacious influence on the acquisition of the virtues. From our relation with God we draw the strength to repel temptations, the self-knowledge to be humble, the gentleness of temper to bear with our neighbors, and the light and the strength with which to practice all the other virtues. Even more can be said, for one may be sure that the virtues not rooted in the interior life are neither solid nor deep. . . .

But the central point of the spiritual life is the contemplative life. Why? Because it is for this that God made us. He made us for himself, that we might know him, love him, and serve him. Hence if we sacrifice ourselves to achieve a betterment of our life and conduct, it is solely that we may render ourselves worthy to be in relationship with God. Thus our interior life is the summit, the ideal, the goal toward which all our efforts ought to converge. . . .

And God in his goodness has desired that even in this life we should exercise ourselves in what will constitute our eternal life: contemplation. Already here below we can contemplate him, although in the mists of faith. Already here below we can love him, and with the same love of heaven, although it does not produce in us the same effects as in the blessed. This is the true life; all else is fading and transitory. For this reason our Lord told Martha that she was concerned about many things when only one thing was necessary and, on the other hand, that Mary had chosen the better part, and that it would never be taken from her (cf. Lk 10:38ff.). In this way our Lord himself teaches us that the contemplative life is better than the active, and that it will never be taken from the soul that has chosen it.

It is the better part because it is the most exalted. To live with God, to know him and to love him, is the highest activity that a creature can exercise. Not even the seraphim can aspire to anything more exalted. It is the better part because it is the most excellent. What is more excellent than to have a relationship with God and to be friends and intimates of the Supreme Being? And no one can take it away from us. The active life is solely of time; the contemplative life is eternal. The life of mortification of the great penitents, the apostolic life of the great apostles, the priestly ministry, no matter how holy and fruitful these may be, end with death. Only one thing does not cease: the contemplative life. It continues in heaven; it is eternal.

Let us see now how in the interior life "the ways of God are not our ways" (cf. Isa 55:8). With this in view we shall find the solution to our problem. We consider the spiritual life according to our own way of thinking, that is, in a very human way. This happens especially in the beginning when we have as yet no experience with it. We imagine that it is a life that always tends upward, in which a person continually ascends and never falls back. And we neglect to consider that the spiritual life, as all human life, must have its peaks and its low points. We think that each day our faults should keep vanishing and that our souls should continue to be purified without ceasing. And indeed our souls do continue to be purified more and more each day, but this purification is one of faith. It is not a tangible purification that we can perceive as in the case of our particular examination of conscience, when we note, for example, that yesterday we had eight faults, today six, tomorrow four, and the day after none.

We think that the spiritual life is one of ever-growing fervor, in which we feel ourselves more enthusiastic, more closely united to our Lord, each day. . . .

But the ways of God are not our ways. I even dare to say that the spiritual life is almost the contrary of what we fancy it. It is true that it goes upward, but by our lowering ourselves. It is true that it purifies the soul, but in the midst of temptations and falls. It is true that its light increases, yet the light is one that is overshadowed with darkness. Therefore, that the light may increase, the darkness must envelop us. That the purification may continue, the most painful temptations must besiege us, and that true fervor may take root in the soul, sensible fervor must frequently forsake us. Thus in the midst of darkness, helplessness, struggles, temptations, and falls, we continue going upward. Yet we do not notice that we are ascending until we arrive at the goal of our aspirations.

— Excerpts from *Secrets of the Interior Life*, pp. 85–88, 122–124

XIII

Secrets of the Interior Life

Sacred Scripture tells us: "For my thoughts are not your thoughts, nor are your ways my ways, says the LORD" (Isa 55:8). Herein is the source of our difficulty in communicating with God, for his thoughts are not our thoughts, nor are his ways our ways. Thus God communicates to us through one way, and we walk in another. He has his manner of approaching us, and we do not understand, for in reality we wish that he would communicate with us in our way. For example, we believe that as often as God communicates with us, we must feel it, since we cannot imagine that communication with a beloved person, as our Lord is, could be dry and barren. But since the ways of God are different from ours, ninety-nine percent of the time when our Lord comes to us, we do not feel it. And this deludes us, and we believe we cannot communicate with our Lord because we cannot perceive him.

To us it seems that our Lord can have only a delicious sweetness, and that when he comes we must, therefore, taste him with the sweetness of the blessed. And sometimes it is thus. The coming of our Lord fills our hearts with sweetness. But God does not always taste the same. He is like the manna; he holds within himself all savors.

Saint Bernadine of Siena says that God has two savors: the savor of sweetness and the savor of bitterness. When we feel our heart heavy, it is also God who draws near. It is Jesus who communicates with us—no matter how poorly we understand that he also possesses the savor of bitterness. Saint Thomas puts it so well in saying that all our errors in the spiritual life flow from our wish to measure divine things with our human criterion, which is so puny and paltry. How often, when we think that we are most distant from God, we are most closely united to him!

According to my view, the secret and key of the interior life is this: Jesus is a hidden God; we must therefore seek him. But in seeking him we must remember that the ways of God are very different from our ways. To know these ways and to seek God through them are the sole means of finding God and of uniting ourselves to him.

———— ❧ ————

Our life is so complex! So very many elements enter into it! We are affected by everything, even by the weather: cold, heat, cloudy days. Hence with greater reason do these various states of our soul affect our being. This fact is especially true in the supernatural order, since God affects us with the most varied invitations of grace, and the devil with his ceaseless solicitations to evil. Again I say: this is the reason why our life is so complex.

Therefore, the wise course is not to analyze those states, but to separate our spiritual life from them in order that nothing and no one may rob us of our treasure, as Saint Paul said: "For I am convinced that neither death, nor life, nor angels, nor rulers, nor things present, nor things to come, nor powers, nor height, nor depth, nor anything else in all creation, will be able to separate us from the love of God in Christ Jesus our Lord" (Rom 8:38). Let us learn how to guard our treasure equally well at midnight and at high noon, whether the tempest is unleashed, or the sun shines brilliantly in a cloudless sky.

— Excerpts from *Secrets of the Interior Life*, pp. 100–101, 149–150

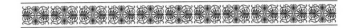

XIV

Transformation in God

According to Saint Bernard, Saint Thomas, and Saint John of the Cross, transformation in God is the final stage of love; consequently it is the summit of holiness. This degree is so exalted that it is proper to heaven. However, God in his mercy and love grants it to some privileged souls on earth. Love is union or a tendency to union. Infinite love is the most perfect union; created love tends to union on earth, and in heaven it will achieve the most perfect union it is capable of, the perfect participation of the all-holy and the all-blessed oneness of God.

To be transformed in God, to be transformed in the Beloved, is to begin to enjoy in this life, that union with

God which constitutes the holiness, glory, and blessedness of the saints. This is the consummation of the union that Christ prayed for to his Father with most ardent desires and petitions on the night of the Last Supper: "I in them and you in me, that they may become completely one" (Jn 17:23). This is also what the Holy Spirit asks for with unspeakable groaning in the souls of those he loves (cf. Rom 8:26). . . .

Love is inexhaustible. In the soul's vocabulary the word "enough" is not found. It has been replaced by this word, "more." "Those who eat of me will hunger for more, and those who drink of me will thirst for more" (Sir 24:21). Love is like that: the greater the fullness, the greater the hunger; the greater the abundance, the greater the thirst.

How is this transformation to be accomplished? Everything in the soul must become divine; everything must be changed into the living image of Christ. . . .

The espoused must be similar to Christ in the soul through a most elevated and most intimate union with the Word of God; a union already exists, but the Word asks for a great union.

The espoused must be similar to Christ in the heart. The heart of Christ is love and sorrow. His heart, like all that he is, is radiant and ruddy, according to the words of the bride in the Song of Songs (cf. Song 5:10); radiant because it is "a reflection of eternal light" (Wis 7:26), ruddy because it is crimsoned with his most precious blood. The heart of Christ is composed of love and of the sorrow which his two great and consuming passions have produced: namely, the glory of God and the salvation of souls. Thus ought to be the heart of the espoused soul.

Such a person's character must also be like that of Christ's: gentle and humble. ". . . [L]earn from me; for I am gentle and humble in heart" (Mt 11:29). The espoused soul's words, actions, deportment, and exterior conduct ought to breathe that attractive humility and that heavenly meekness of Christ. And this ought to be to such an extent that others would discern Christ whenever they would approach that person, who would be diffusing the good aroma of Christ (cf. 2 Cor 2:15) on all sides, attracting everyone with the fragrance of its perfumes.

Finally, the espoused soul must be similar to Christ in his or her flesh. "Always carrying in the body the death of Jesus, so that the life of Jesus may also be made visible in our bodies. For while we live, we are always being given up to death for Jesus's sake, so that the life of Jesus may be made visible in our mortal flesh" (2 Cor 4:10). In this way the soul is akin to the afflicted body of Christ on earth until the day comes when he or she will be like his glorious body in heaven, according to that text of Saint Paul: "But our citizenship is in heaven, and it is from there that we are expecting a Savior, the Lord Jesus Christ. He will transform the body of our humiliation that it may be conformed to the body of his glory" (Phil 3:20). . . .

. . . [W]herever Christ is, he is formed by the Holy Spirit. Wherever Christ is, he is also, and for the same reason, conceived in a certain manner by the Blessed Virgin Mary. Let the soul call upon that most tender Mother. Let the soul invoke her that with her powerful intercession she may obtain the soul's perfect transformation into Christ. The espoused soul ought to ask for this transformation. It is pleasing to God that we ask for and desire the very grace that he wishes to give us, especially when this grace is that of union, when the gift that we beseech is he himself.

So let the soul that is united with the Word ask with insistence from the Holy Spirit for this supreme grace, which is the highest degree of perfection and of holiness, the ultimate degree of union and of love, the supreme degree of happiness.

— Excerpts from *Secrets of the Interior Life*, pp. 193–197, 201–202

XV

The Blessed Virgin

God's most humble creature, after the holy humanity of Christ, is the Blessed Virgin. She has understood better than anyone else the immensity of the blessings she received from God. Her Magnificat is a canticle of humility as well as of gratitude and love. The Virgin herself is the author of her own panegyric, one that has never been surpassed by creatures, glorifying God and rejoicing in her Savior, because he has done great things in her, he who is mighty and whose name is holy. Furthermore, does not experience teach that all God's favors are such as to humble and confound us? This self-abnegation is the very essence of humility, love, and adoration.

Nor need privileged souls be too greatly concerned about not corresponding to grace. To be sure, whoever looks upon one's own nothingness has great reason to fear. But if that person instead gazes on the goodness and the love of God, what is there to fear? God gives "both to will and to accomplish" (cf. Phil 2:13); yes, even correspondence with grace is a gift of God. Whoever confides in him will never be confounded. And God, who enriches the soul with the treasures of his love, will cause the soul to know how to profit from them.

———————

The most holy Virgin gives us this same teaching when she says that God did great things in her, "for he has looked with favor on the lowliness of his servant" (Lk 2:48). Perhaps we think that the Blessed Virgin says this out of humility. There is no doubt about it whatever. But she speaks the truth precisely because she is humble. And truly in her our Lord met with the only qualities that he cannot help but meet with in all creatures: lowliness and nothingness.

Perhaps we believe that what attracted our Lord to the most holy Virgin was her purity and her humility. No. Purity, humility, and all the graces that the Blessed Virgin received came after the love of God. God first loved her, and because he loved her, he enriched her with so many graces. Hence what he saw in Mary before all these virtues, graces, and spiritual riches is what he sees in all creation, which of itself is nothing more than lowliness and nothingness: "for he has looked with favor on the lowliness of his servant."

— Excerpts from *Secrets of the Interior Life*, pp. 182, 49

Notes

1. See Chapter IX of the present work.

2. See Chapter VI of the present work.

3. The Word or *Logos*, that is, the second Person of the Trinity, who became incarnate.

Sources

Martinez, Luis Maria. *The Sanctifier*, Boston: Pauline Books & Media, 2003.

_____. *Secrets of the Interior Life*, St. Louis, MO: B. Herder Book Company, 1949.

_____. *Only Jesus*, St. Louis, MO: B. Herder Book Company, 1962.

Pauline
BOOKS & MEDIA

The Daughters of St. Paul operate book and media centers at the following addresses. Visit, call, or write the one nearest you today, or find us on the World Wide Web, www.pauline.org.

CALIFORNIA

3908 Sepulveda Blvd, Culver City, CA 90230	310-397-8676
935 Brewster Avenue, Redwood City, CA 94063	650-369-4230
5945 Balboa Avenue, San Diego, CA 92111	858-565-9181

FLORIDA

145 S.W. 107th Avenue, Miami, FL 33174	305-559-6715

HAWAII

1143 Bishop Street, Honolulu, HI 96813	808-521-2731
Neighbor Islands call:	866-521-2731

ILLINOIS

172 North Michigan Avenue, Chicago, IL 60601	312-346-4228

LOUISIANA

4403 Veterans Memorial Blvd, Metairie, LA 70006	504-887-7631

MASSACHUSETTS

885 Providence Hwy, Dedham, MA 02026	781-326-5385

MISSOURI

9804 Watson Road, St. Louis, MO 63126	314-965-3512

NEW YORK

64 W. 38th Street, New York, NY 10018	212-754-1110

PENNSYLVANIA

Philadelphia—relocating	215-676-9494

SOUTH CAROLINA

243 King Street, Charleston, SC 29401	843-577-0175

VIRGINIA

1025 King Street, Alexandria, VA 22314	703-549-3806

CANADA

3022 Dufferin Street, Toronto, ON M6B 3T5	416-781-9131

¡También somos su fuente para libros,
videos y música en español!